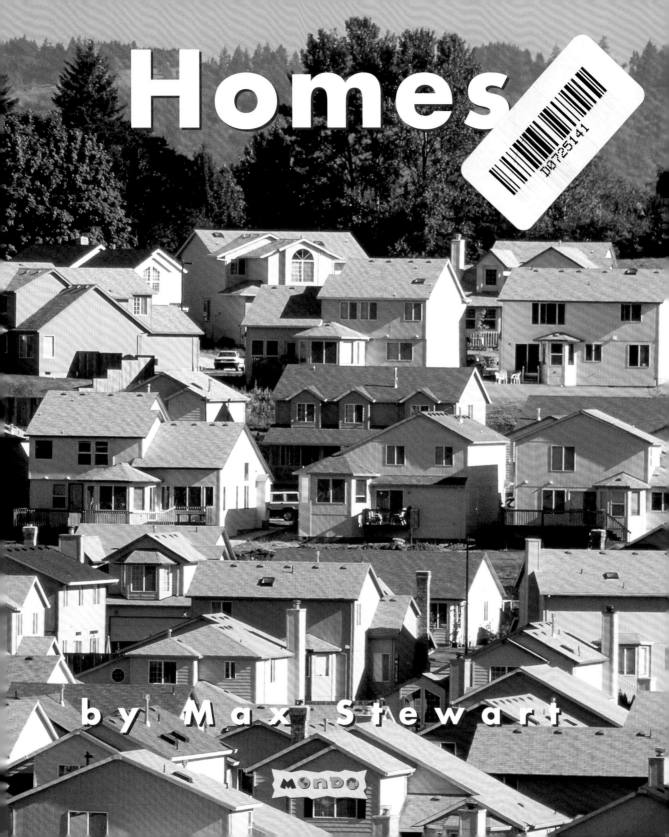

Homes

by Max Stewart

This is a home.
It is in the forest.

This is a home.
It is on the island.

This is a home.
It is in the city.

This is a home.
It is on the mountain.

This is a home.
It is on the water.

This is a home.
It is on the beach.

This is a home.
It is in the desert.